This book belongs to
a very special girl
who is amazing and true: you!

_____

(your name here)

May you always
reach for the stars.

Also by Ashley Rice

For an Incredible Kid
Girl Power
You Are a Girl Who Totally Rocks!
You Go, Girl... Keep Dreaming

Library of Congress Control Number: 2010914533
ISBN: 978-1-59842-598-7

Blue Mountain Press is registered in U.S. Patent and Trademark Office.
Certain trademarks are used under license.

Printed in China.
First printing of this edition: 2011

Blue Mountain Arts, Inc.
P.O. Box 4549, Boulder, Colorado 80306

Girls
Rule

a very special book
created especially for girls

updated edition

Ashley Rice

Blue Mountain Press ™

Boulder, Colorado

Introduction

Hi, my name is Penelope J. Miller, and I am the narrator of this book. You might know me from the first edition of *Girls Rule*, a book that has been read by girls all over the world. Now I'm here in the updated edition of the book, which has lots of new, inspiring words and drawings to help you through all your adventures of being a girl in the world. If you read the first book, welcome back! If you didn't, it's nice to meet you!

This book was created with the purpose of keeping you posted on all the possibilities that are out there and to remind you how valued and talented you are. You'll find encouraging words about how to accomplish great things, look toward the future, and be happy being you, plus some important lessons on life that every girl should know.

You are amazing and have lots of wonderful things to offer the world. To put it simply: you rule. Always remember that, and you will go far. You've got everything inside yourself that you need to be the best you can be. You just have to believe in yourself, be yourself, and embrace the world and everything it has to offer, always knowing in your heart that you can do and be anything you want to.

So wherever you are and whatever you're doing, I hope you have a great day and that all your dreams come true!

Your friend,
Penelope J.

Girls Rule

Girls who rule
don't ever sell themselves short
in any sort of way...
They search for the right answers
and do whatever it takes
to follow their paths.
They fight for their own truths
(even in those times when
their hearts are breaking).
They find their own bright way,
and they can get through anything.
They are AMAZING!

Come with me and see
how amazing you really are.
Let's look at all the things
you do that make a difference.
Let's celebrate your uniqueness
and your independent, creative spirit
and your kindness.
Let's take a moment to remember
how special you are
and how truly unique
your gifts are to this world.

There is greatness in every girl, and you're no exception. You can take on the world and succeed in so many different directions. You've got your own ideas of what it means to be real and free and to have tons of fun. You get the work done when it needs to be done. You're incredible and outstanding and excellent in so many ways...

And your future is going to be even better than you can imagine.

In This World...

In this world,
there is only one
you.

You have your
very own ways.

You've got your own
walking shoes
in this world.

You are the
only one who
smiles and laughs
exactly as you do.

You are the
only one who lives
and thinks exactly
as you do.

You are your
very own you.
You've got your
own dreams and
your ideas, too...

In this world,
there is only one
you.

A Girl like You

She is a girl who changes minds, takes chances, turns heads, listens. She is the first to arrive, the last to leave, the first to lend a hand. She is a girl who remembers, pauses, makes an effort, laughs. She is unique, irreplaceable, real. That girl is... you!

Girl, you've got
the dreams
to take you wherever
you need to go.
You've got
all the answers you need.
You've got questions
that will take you
on unexpected journeys.
You've got wisdom
and a love of life and magic.
Girl, you've got the power
to make your dreams come true!

How to be a rock star, prizewinner, teacher, astrophysicist, novelist, professional wrestler, actor, painter, radio personality, editor, filmmaker, guitar player, columnist, astronaut, singer, designer, cartoonist, inventor, architect, builder, producer, writer, athlete, artist, programmer, dancer, technician, or stylist

in one step or less...

1. GO FOR it!

You Can Do Anything

If anyone tries to tell you that you can't work hard enough to face the task in front of you — show them that you're tough. If anyone tries to tell you that you are not that strong, don't listen to discouragement — know that you belong.

If anyone tries to tell you that you can't sing your own song or make your way in the world...

PROVE them wRong.

Follow Your Dreams

Many people speak of dreams as fanciful things, like fairies and charmed rings and lands of enchantment. Others only believe in faraway dreams, such as stars or sea castles with elf-like inhabitants.

There are day dreamers and night dreamers who dream up make-believe places. They use much imagination, and in that way, they are dream gifted. But the serious dreamers are those who catch dreams and bring them to life to show that when they were dreaming, they meant it.

Hold on to your dreams;
they are as precious as
laughter — they are
eternal, like stars.

dreams

You Are a Lover of Words...
One Day, You Will
Write a Book

People turn to you because you give voice to dreams, notice little things, and make otherwise impossible imaginings appear real. You are a rare bird who thinks the world is beautiful enough to try to figure it out, who has the courage to dive into your wild mind and go swimming there.

You are someone who still believes in cloud watching, people watching, daydreaming, tomorrow, favorite colors, silver clouds, dandelions, and sorrow. Be sacred. Be cool. Be wild. Go far. Words do more than plant miracle seeds. With you writing them, they can change the world.

Don't be afraid to be a little different.
Your uniqueness is one of the most
incredible things about you.
Get to know yourself
and have clear goals and dreams
to keep you motivated
when things get tough.

Have confidence in yourself
and find creative solutions
to any problems
you might encounter.
Just be yourself...
you're already great!

One day, you will find that all the daydreams you planted when you were small have blossomed into giant sunflowers. One day, you will turn around and see the world at your front door. One day, you will move mountains and write your name across the sky.

A Few Lessons on Life from Me (Penelope)...

On Being Great

Being great means expressing your individuality with confidence and honesty. It means standing up for yourself and finding your way through adversity with creative solutions. Being great means knowing how to accept criticism and benefit from it and not be discouraged by it.

Being great means putting your best foot forward, giving it your best shot, being yourself at all times, and never giving up.

On Courage

Courage is the ability to face
up to your fears.
Courage is lending a
helping hand.
Courage is attempting
to understand all sides
of a situation.
Sometimes, courage is having
the guts to go.
Sometimes, courage is having
the guts to stay.
Courage can be lots of things,
and it can be played out
in many different ways.
And you?
You've had courage all along.

Always be courageous, especially when the stakes are against you or you've got a hard road ahead of you. Always be courageous, especially when the road is long and you've got a ways to go. Always be courageous, especially when people are challenging you and your personal beliefs.

Always be courageous,
and you can never go wrong.

On Leaving

When you are getting
ready to leave a place...

there are a few things
you can do to make yourself
feel less nervous...

 pack a teddy bear...

a few happy snapshots...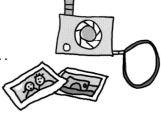

and your favorite book
to keep you steady.

Remember to say goodbye
to everyone...

 and to any special places
there that are close to
your heart.

P.S. If you think you are too old for a teddy
bear, you can pack something else in place
of it, but the truth is: no one is ever really
too old for a teddy bear.

When You
Go Out There...

Take care
of yourself

make wise
choices

go to sleep
at a decent hour

eat your
vegetables!

Be brave

stand tall

make good friends

trust yourself

give it your all!

On Friendship

Through the years,
the tears, the smiles,
the miles...
and all the things
that happened
while we were out there
chasing our dreams...

In the end,
friends are what
matter most.

Friends are angels sent
down to earth to make
good days and to help
us find our way.

A True Friend

A friend is someone you turn to when you have no place to go… but a true friend is someone you want to stop and talk to when you have a million places to be. A friend is someone who tells you it will be okay… a true friend is someone who stays with you or calls until it is. A friend is like a day of fine, fine weather… A true friend reminds you that some days… the sky can be blue (even if it isn't right then).

A friend will meet you at the finish line… A true friend lights the way.

There's nothing like a little help from your friends.

On Love

The strange thing about love is that it can make your heart beat faster, and the strange thing about love is that it can make you laugh and then cry. The strange thing about love is that it's uneven: in this life, you may be loved by someone you don't love back, and you may love someone who doesn't return your love.

The strange thing about love is that it's always worth it. The strange thing about love is that it is always there somewhere in your life. The strange thing about love is that you have to believe in it for it to be true, and the strange thing about love is that even if it's a different story than you expected, somehow it all works out.

Love is strange, isn't it? But trust in it... and you will be all right.

Love starts out small.
It grows bigger every day.
Love will make you kind.
It will make you brave.
Love will teach you things
you never thought you'd know.

So always treat love like a dream:
hold on tight... and never let it go.

Be Strong and Listen to Your Heart

When there are way too many dust bunnies under your bed... when your week's way too busy and then suddenly seems empty... when your computer is driving you mad... when you miss the bus or can't find a ride and you arrive late (again, again)...

When it seems like most of the people you know seem to change too fast or to come and go... the best thing to do is to take a walk or draw a simple picture with crayons or sit outside under a tree and look at the moon.

Sometimes you just need to take a minute to breathe and reflect before returning to face the spinning world. It helps you go back out there with strength, hope, and love in your heart (always).

The solution to any problem is right inside your heart. It may be hard to see at first, but it becomes easier once you start.

Look around you and begin the journey of your own life today. Listen hard, and no matter where "there" is, your heart will take you where you need to be — much sooner than you think!

Just a Few Words About You...

amazing

unique

wise

awesome

funny

true

excellent

kind

understanding

talented   strong

brave

super   brilliant

outstanding

incredible

extraordinary

unforgettable

sweet

Incredible Changes Lie Ahead!

These days, everything may be changing around you (including your body and your clothes and what you learn and how much you grow). Just remember...

Everything changes: the seasons,
    the waves and the seas,
the mountains, the leaves on the trees.
Everything changes: our lives lived
    beneath the stars...
what we keep in our pockets,
how we know where we are.
Everything changes: from the time to
    the weather...
but by honoring your courage, individuality,
    flexibility, and creativity,
you can ride through these changes, too...

You will always have
your same strong
and true character
on which to rely.

Everything changes...
but change can be good!

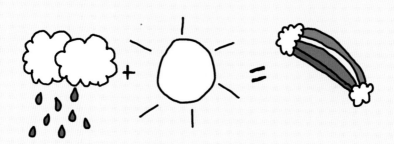

Take a Break

Take some time just for yourself.
Feel the warmth of sunshine on your face,
and feel the touch of wind in your hair.
Concentrate on all that is good in life.
Think of all you've accomplished
and everything you've done
to get where you are today.
Celebrate life's possibilities
and everything
each new day has to offer.

Take a Bath

Taking a bath won't change anything, but...
when you are in the bathtub, you are not
responsible for anything — you are wet,
for example, so no one can ask you to do
anything... you can't do homework in there,
because your papers will get wet... you
can't read any e-mail... or work on any
assignments... or return any messages...
or do any chores... or...

Maybe it should be
a long bath.

Don't think that it's such a terrible thing to get sad or down or to stop believing in sunshine for a while. Don't worry too much if you feel empty or lost or you can't make yourself want to smile.

Don't think that it's not okay to
want to sit a day out or to be
scared or tired or blue. Everybody
gets sad sometimes. And crying and
hurting — just like laughing and
dreaming — are just things that
people do.

This is your guardian angel saying
that even if things seem a little bit
crazy where you are right now,
from up here you look pretty good...

That tangled mess that's
got you worried — it's
just a dark cloud...

and there's a rainbow
on the other side.

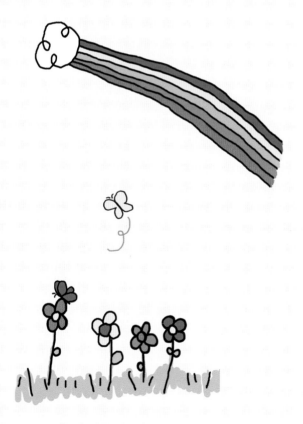

Six Steps for a Great Day

1. Have fun.

2. Do what you like to do.

3. Know that the key
   to your happiness
   lies in your own hands.

4. Be happy, healthy, and wise.

5. Live like there is no
   tomorrow or yesterday.

6. With truth, love, humor, honor, and courage, make your own way into the sunshine.

Your Star

There is a star in the sky... just for you.
That star will make sure that your dreams come true.

So in case you are stumbling – don't get too blue.
That star in the sky... it believes in you.

And in case you were
wondering...

I do, too.

(I believe in you and
your star.)

Always Walk in the Sunshine

Whenever you're having a hard time
or you're feeling down
or things aren't going your way...
walk in the sunshine.
It will help you find
the hope for something better.
For there, in the sunshine,
you can best imagine and act upon
your greatest hopes and dreams —
and follow through.

So... no matter what you do,
even when clouds surround you...
always walk in the sunshine.

You are a very
special star in this
world...

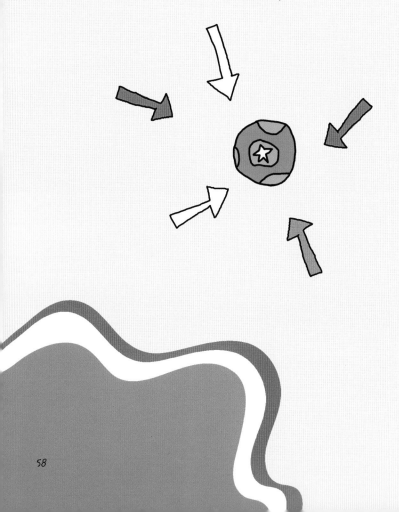

...go on and shine
go on and shine
go on and
shine.

May your dreams
soar like kites.

May your hopes
fly high.

May you smile often
and love like there
is no tomorrow.

May all your tomorrows
be magic.

May you have
the very best of everything —
big hopes, fun dreams,
and many great and
excellent days.

May you have incomparable moments,
memories, and lots of
triumphs, hopes,
love,
smiles,
and grins from the
sparkling stars above.

Keep Being You

Every day... take good care of yourself.
Lend a grin to someone else.
Don't let any bad things that happen
   make you frown.
Look outside at the world
   around you.
Sparkle and shine.
Look up at the sky.
Stay hopeful, brave, and true.

Every day,
just keep being you...
a girl who rules.

You are a
very special girl...

Just make sure
you always
remember that.